Listen to the exhortation of the
dawn!
Look to this day for it is life,
The very life of life!
In its brief course lie all the
verities
And all the realities
Of your existence;
The bliss of growth,
The glory of action,
The splendor of beauty;
For yesterday is but a dream
And tomorrow is only a vision;
But today well lived
Makes every yesterday
A dream of happiness
And every tomorrow
A vision of hope.
Look well, therefore, to this day!
Such is the salutation of the dawn.

FROM THE SANSKRIT

Most people love humanity.
It is the person next door they
can't stand.

We make a living by what we get
and live by what we give.

You are my mirror wherein I see
Myself—as I am, and as I should
        be.
I talk and you listen—that's all
        you do,
And yet I see in the eyes of you
The pattern of life fall into place—
The truth reflected in your face.
                    H.L. MARSHALL

Wisdom of Words

Selected by
Peg Huxtable

Illustrated by
Jan Gallehawk

**SELECT
EDITIONS**

ISBN: 1 86476 014 1

Help me to be
Cheerful when things go wrong;
Persevering when things are
difficult; and serene when things
are irritating.

Enable me to be
Helpful to those in difficulties;
Kind to those in need;
Sympathetic to those whose hearts
are sore and sad.

I thought I heard the voice of God,
And climbed the highest steeple.
But God declared, 'Go down
again,
I dwell among the people.'

You are a Christian today
because somebody cared.
Now it's your turn.
                    WARREN W. WIERSBE

If absence makes the heart grow
fonder,
Then some people really love
church.

*Keep praying, but be thankful
that God's answers are wiser
than your prayers.*

*The two greatest days in a
person's life are the day he was
born and the day he finds out why.
he was born.*

*At his fiftieth wedding anniversary
Henry Ford was asked,
'What is the formula for a good
marriage?'
He replied: 'The same as for a
successful car; stick to one
model.'*

Hope is the mechanism that keeps the human race tenaciously alive, dreaming, planning, building. Hope is not the opposite of realism.... it is the opposite of cynicism and despair.

ARDETH WHITEMAN

In our era the road to holiness necessarily passes through the world of action.

DAG HAMMARSKJOLD

The true test of character is not how much we know how to do, but how we behave when we don't know what to do.

*The day the child realises that all
adults are imperfect he becomes
an adolescent. The day he
forgives them he becomes an
adult. The day he forgives himself
he becomes wise.*

*The happiness of life is made up
of minute fractions.
The little soon forgotten charities
of a kiss or smile, a kind look,
a heartfelt compliment—
Countless infinitesimals
of pleasurable and genial feelings.*
        SAMUEL TAYLOR COLERIDGE

When it comes to generosity,
some people stop at nothing.

The Bible is the one book to which
any thoughtful person may go with
any honest question of life or
destiny and find the answer of
God by honest searching.

I am only one, but I am one.
I cannot do everything
but I can do something;
and what I can do,
that I ought to do;
and what I ought to do,
by the grace of God I shall do.
                              EDWARD E. HALE

*God is a sure paymaster,
though he does not always
pay at the end of the week.*
                    C. H. SPURGEON

Do not pray by heart but with
heart.

*It is usually not so much
the greatness of our
trouble as the littleness
of our spirit which makes
us complain.*
                    JEREMY TAYLOR

*Watches, cars and Christians
can all look good and shiny.
But watches don't tick, cars
don't go and Christians don't
make a difference without insides.
For a Christian, that's the
Holy Spirit.*

TIM DOWNS

*You can make more friends
in two months by becoming
interested in other people,
than you can in two years
by trying to get other people
interested in you.*

DALE CARNEGIE

Notice in an English country
church bulletin:
*'Due to the high cost of
maintaining the church, it would
be appreciated if parishioners
would cut the grass around their
own graves.'*

*Never look for the faults as you go
through life, and even when you
find them, it is right and kind
to be somewhat blind, and look
for the virtues behind them.*

*Money buys everything except
love, personality, freedom, and
immortality.*

If all pulled in one direction the world would keel over.

HANNAN J. AYALTI
Yiddish proverb

If man is only a little lower than the angels, the angels should reform.

MARY WILSON LITTLE

The worst moment for an aetheist is when he feels grateful and doesn't know who to thank.

WENDY WARD

Perhaps the straight and narrow path would be wider if more people used it.

KAY INGRAM

When you want to believe in something you also have to believe in everything that's necessary for believing in it.

UGO BETTI

Lots of people think they are charitable if they give away their old clothes and things they don't want.

MYRTLE REED

Feel for others in your own pocket.
        CHARLES HADDON SPURGEON

Difficult as it is really to listen to someone in affliction, it is just as difficult for him to know that compassion is listening to him.
        SIMONE WEIL

You cannot make yourself feel something you do not feel, but you can make yourself do right in spite of your feelings.
        PEARL S. BUCK

Man thinks of himself as a creator instead of a user and this delusion is robbing him, not only of his natural heritage, but perhaps of his future.

HELEN HOOVER

No one fails when they do their best.

When you feel you must complain,
        smile.
Do not care if things seem gray.
Soon there will come a brighter
        day.
You will find that it will pay to
        smile.

God be in my head, and in my
* understanding;*
God be in my eyes, and in my
* looking;*
God be in my mouth, and in my
* speaking;*
God be in my heart, and in my
* thinking;*
God be at my end, and at my
* departing.*

SARUM MISSAL

The nature of God is a circle,
Of which the circle is everywhere
and the circumference is nowhere.

If there is righteousness in the
heart,
There will be beauty in the
character.
If there is beauty in the character,
There will be harmony in the
home,
There will be order in the nation,
There will be peace in the world.

The best reflections are there
when the wind, water and you are
still.

PEG HUXTABLE

To everything there is a season,
and a time to every purpose under
        heaven:
a time to be born, and a time to
        die;
a time to plant, and a time to
        pluck up that which is
        planted ...
a time to love, and a time to hate;
a time of war and a time of peace.
        ECCLESIASTES 3:1, 2 & 8.

I have only just a minute,
Only sixty seconds in it,
Forced upon me, can't refuse it,
Didn't seek it, didn't choose it,
But it's up to me to use it,
I must suffer if I lose it,
Give account if I abuse it,
But Eternity is in it.

Take therefore no thought for the morrow; for the morrow shall take thought for the things of itself. Sufficient unto the day is the evil thereof.

MATTHEW 6:34.

I have to live with myself, and so, I want to be fit for myself to know.

*It is a good thing to be rich,
And a good thing to be strong,
But it is a better thing
To be loved by many friends.*

Two men trod the way of life;
The first, with downcast eye;
The second with an eager face
Uplifted to the sky.
He who gazed upon the ground
        said, 'Life is dull and gray,'
But he who looked into the stars
Went singing on his way.

I believe in the sun even when it is
        not shining.
I believe in love even when I feel it
        not.
I believe in God even when he
        seems to be silent.

*We share our happiness with each
   other—
   and it becomes greater.
We share our troubles with each
   other—
   and they become smaller.
We share one another's griefs and
   burdens—
   and their weight becomes
   possible to bear.*

*In giving and receiving
we learn to love and be loved;
we encounter the meaning of life,
the mystery of existence.*

The careful balance between silence and words, withdrawal and involvement, distance and closeness, solitude and community forms a good basis for a wonderful shared life.

Character, like a well-cut jewel, shines which ever way it is approached.

J.C. GEIKE

No one ever ruined their eyesight by looking on the bright side.

Our deeds travel with us from afar, and what we have been makes us what we are.

GEORGE ELIOT

The desert bears the sign of man's complete helplessness as he can do nothing to subsist alone and by himself, and thus he discovers his weaknesses and the necessity of seeking help and strength in God.

RENE VOILLAUME

To err is human, to persist in error is devilish.

ST AUGUSTINE OF HIPPO

The more of doubt, the stronger the faith, I say, if faith overcomes doubt.

ROBERT BROWNING

A life spent making mistakes is not only more honourable but more useful than a life spent doing nothing.

GEORGE BERNARD SHAW

It is by forgiving that one is forgiven.

MOTHER TERESA

We all like to forgive and we all love best not those who offend us least, nor those who have done most for us, but those who make it most easy for us to forgive them.
SAMUEL BUTLER

Don't walk in front of me;
I may not follow.
Don't walk behind me,
I may not lead.
Walk beside me;
And just be my friend.
ALBERT CAMUS

Anxieties yield at a negative rate
Increasing in smallness the longer
they wait.

Who walks in a rut walks alone
Ruts grow deeper and deeper:
There's only room for one in a rut,
Walls rise steep and steeper.
Soon he's lonely lost to view,
Soon he can't see over
To where his friends of yesterday
Are walking in fields of clover.

Friends are God's apology for relations.

HUGH KINGSMILL

I believe that God is in me as the sun is in the colour and fragrance of a flower—the light in my darkness, the Voice in my Silence.

HELEN KELLER

Goodness does not more certainly make men happy than happiness makes them good.

WALTER SAVAGE

The purpose of words is to convey ideas. When the ideas are grasped, the words are forgotten. Where can I find a man who has forgotten words?
He is the one I would like to talk to.

CHUANG TZU

The belief in immortality rests not very much on the hope of going on. Few of us want to do that, but we would like very much to begin again.

HEYWOOD BROUN

Mother to six-year-old:
'Jane, what are you doing?'
'I'm drawing God.'
'But darling, nobody knows what
God looks like.'
'No mummy, they don't yet, but
they will when they've seen my
drawing.'
                    ROBERT LLEWELYN

All too often modern man becomes
the plaything of his circumstances
because he no longer has any
leisure time; he doesn't know how
to provide himself with the leisure
he needs to stop to take a good
look at himself.
                    MICHEL QUOIST

Life is rather like a tin of sardines—we are all looking for the key.

ALAN BENNETT

Some great spiritual teachers thought life was rather like a waiting room. It's certainly not your eternal home, but there is no reason why you shouldn't make yourself as comfortable as you can before you get there.

RABBI LIONEL BLUE

God give me work
Till my life shall end.
And life
Till my work is done.
    ON WINIFRED HOLTBY'S GRAVE

Love gives nought but itself and
    takes naught but from itself.
Love possesses not, nor would it
    be possessed.
For love is sufficient unto love.
                KAHLIL GIBRAN

I have found the paradox that if I love until it hurts, then there is no hurt, but only more love.
                    MOTHER TERESA

A miracle is an event which creates faith. Frauds deceive. An event which creates faith does not deceive; therefore it is not a fraud, but a miracle.
                    GEORGE BERNARD SHAW

Mourning is not forgetting. It is an undoing.
Every minute tie has to be untied and something permanent and valuable recovered and assimilated from the dust.
                    MARGERY ALLINGHAM

Nature has some perfections to show that she is in the image of God, and some defects to show that she is only his image.
                    BLAISE PASCAL

O Lord, Thou knowest how busy I
must be this day;
If I forget Thee, do not Thou forget
me.

SIR JACOB ASTLEY

To begin with oneself, but not to
end with oneself;
To start from oneself, but not to
aim at oneself;
To comprehend oneself, but not to
be preoccupied with oneself.

MARTIN BUBER

This above all—to thine own self
    be true,
And it must follow, as the night the
    day,
Thou canst not then be false to
    any man.
                WILLIAM SHAKESPEARE
                        from Hamlet

Small child asks, 'Why are we
here on earth Mummy?'
Mother answers, 'To help others'.
Small child: 'Why are the others
here?'

If all the good people were clever,
And all clever people were good,
The world would be nicer than
  ever
We thought that it possibly could.
But somehow, 'tis seldom or never
The two hit it off as they should;
The good are so harsh to the
  clever,
The clever so rude to the good.
    ELIZABETH WORDSWORTH

The Indian sees no need for
setting apart one day in seven as a
holy day, since to him all days are
God's.
    CHARLES EASTMAN

*The only difference between a
saint and a sinner is that every
saint has a past and every sinner
has a future.*

OSCAR WILDE

*Should we all confess our sins to
one another we would all laugh at
one another for our lack of
originality.*

KAHLIL GIBRAN

*We would often be sorry if our
wishes were granted.*

AESOP

Conformity is one of the most fundamental dishonesties of all. When we reject our specialness, water down our God-given individuality and uniqueness, we begin to lose our freedom. The conformist is in no way a free man. He has to follow the herd.

NORMAN VINCENT PEALE

When life seems difficult and the road ahead is steep, remember God didn't make the earth flat, and it is more interesting and beautiful because of that.

PEG HUXTABLE

*For some people religion is like
an artificial limb.
It has neither warmth nor life; and
although it helps them to stumble
along, it never becomes part of
them.
It must be strapped on each day.*

*Do all the good you can,
By all the means you can,
In all the ways you can,
In all the places you can,
At all the times you can,
To all the people you can,
As long as ever you can.*

JOHN WESLEY

A FEW THOUGHTS ON THE LORD'S PRAYER

*I cannot pray **our**, if my faith has no room for others and their need.*
*I cannot pray **who art in heaven**, if all my interests and pursuits are in earthly things.*
*I cannot pray **hallowed be thy name**, if I am not striving, with God's help, to be holy.*
*I cannot pray **thy kingdom come**, if I am unwilling or resentful of having it in my life.*
*I cannot pray **on earth as it is in heaven**, unless I am truly ready to give myself to God's service here and now.*

*I cannot pray **give us this day our daily bread**, without expending honest effort for it, or if I would withold from my neighbour the bread that I receive.*

*I cannot pray **forgive us our trespasses as we forgive those who trespass against us**, if I continue to harbour a grudge against anyone.*

*I cannot pray **lead us not into temptation**, if I deliberately choose to remain in a situation where I am likely to be tempted.*

*I cannot pray **deliver us from evil**, if I am not prepared to fight evil with my life and my prayer.*

*I cannot pray **thine is the kingdom**, if I am unwilling to obey him.*

*I cannot pray **thine is the power and the glory**, if I am seeking power for myself and my own glory first.*

*I cannot pray **forever and ever**, if I am too anxious about each day's affairs.*

*I cannot pray **amen**, unless I honestly say,*

'Cost what it may, this is my prayer.'

The world is moving so fast these days that the person who says it can't be done is generally interrupted by someone doing it.
HARRY EMERSON FOSDICK

Everyone is enthusiastic at times. Some have enthusiasm for thirty minutes, others have it for thirty days—but it is the person that has it for thirty years who makes a success of life.

Let nothing disturb you, let nothing frighten you; everything passes away except God; God alone is sufficient.

ST THERESA

Real love is the universal language—understood by all. You may have every accomplishment or give your body to be burned, but, if love is lacking, all this will profit you and the cause of Christ nothing.

HENRY DRUMMOND

A pessimist is one who makes difficulties of his opportunities; an optimist is one who makes opportunities of his difficulties.

REGINALD B. MANSELL

There are no 'white' or 'coloured'
signs on the foxholes or
graveyards of battle.
                    JOHN F. KENNEDY

The Bible is alive, it speaks to me;
it has feet, it runs after me;
it has hands, it lays hold on me.
                    MARTIN LUTHER

Fear knocked at the door.
Faith answered.
No-one was there.

*There is so much good in the
        worst of us
And so much bad in the best of us
To find fault with the rest of us.*

*There are four things you can do
with the hurts that come into your
life. Nurse them, curse them,
rehearse them, or reverse them.*
                    PATRICK SHAUGHNESSY

*There is a past which has gone
forever, but there is a future which
is still our own.*

*A real pessimist looks at a
doughnut and sees only the hole.*

*Experiences is what you've got
when you're too old to use it.*

*Always ask a busy man when you
want a job done well. The others
haven't the time.*

The way we respond to criticism pretty much depends on the way we respond to praise. But if praise deflates us, then criticism will build us up. But if praise inflates us, then criticism will crush us. Both responses leads to defeat.

WARREN W. WIERSBE

It is easy to be tolerant when you do not care.

C. F. ROGERS

The only people who achieve much, are those who want knowledge so badly, that they seek it while the conditions are still unfavourable. Favourable conditions never come.

Those who expect to reap the blessings of freedom must undergo the fatigue of supporting it.
                    THOMAS PAINE

The real measure of our wealth is how much we'd be worth, if we lost all our money.
JOHN HENRY JOWETT

Happiness adds and multiplies as we divide it with others.

Wise men talk because they have something to say. Fools talk because they must say something.
PLATO

A pessimist is one who blows out the light to see how dark it is.

When you come to the end of your rope. Tie a knot in it and hold on.

You'll never get rid of a bad temper by losing it.

On a Wayside Pulpit
"Come in for your free faith lift!"
(try to say that quickly)

What shall it profit a man, if he gain the whole world and lose his own soul?

JESUS CHRIST

We cannot tell the precise moment when friendship is formed.

Faith is putting all your eggs in God's basket. Then counting your blessings before they hatch.
ROMONA C. CARROLL

More important than length of life,
is how we spend each day.
                    MARIE A. FURTADO

As in filling a cup drop by drop,
there is at last a drop which makes
it run over. So in a series of kind-
nesses, there is at last one which
makes it run over.
                    SAMUEL JOHNSON

If you read history, you will find
that Christians who did the most
for the present world, were those
who thought the most of the next.
                    C. S. LEWIS

He that is good at making excuses,
is seldom good at anything else.
                    BENJAMIN FRANKLIN

Try praising your wife even if it
does frighten her first.

When a person forgives another
he is promising to do three things
about the intending wrong doing;
not to use it against the wrong
doer in the future; not to talk
about it to others; and not to dwell
on it himself.

Don't put off for tomorrow what you can do today, because if you enjoyed it today, you can do it again tomorrow.

The enlightened care more about living than winning.

Those who say it can't be done, shouldn't stand in the way of those who are doing it.

We cannot resist change, but we can choose the direction of change.

KENNON CALLAHAN

For a man who cannot wonder is but a pair of spectacles behind which there are no eyes.

THOMAS CARLYLE

Duty makes us do things well, but love makes us do them beautifully.

REV PHILLIP BROOKS

Happiness grows at our own firesides, and is not to be picked in stranger's gardens.

DOUGLAS JERROLD

Men go forth to wonder at the height of mountains, the huge waves of the sea, the broad flow of the ocean, the course of the stars and forget to wonder at themselves.

AUGUSTINE

The best place to be is here.
The best time to be here is now.

Today everything is possible
Yesterday has gone.

We do not what we ought,
What we ought not, we do,
And lean upon the thought
That chance will bring us through.
                    MATTHEW ARNOLD

Common sense is the most widely
shared commodity in the world,
for every man is convinced that he
is well supplied with it.

'I can forgive but I cannot forget.'
is only another way of saying
'I cannot forgive.'
            HENRY WARD BEECHER

If God did not exist, it would be
necessary to invent him.
            VOLTAIRE

There is only one thing in the
world worse than being talked
about, and that is not being talked
about.
            OSCAR WILDE

If we might have a second chance
To live the days once more,
And rectify mistakes we've made
To even up the score.

If we might have a second chance
To use the knowledge gained,
Perhaps we might become at last
As fine as God ordained.

But though we can't retrace our
steps,
However stands the score,
Tomorrow brings another chance,
For us to try one more.

Mercy is Love being gracious.
Eloquence is Love talking.
Prophecy is Love foretelling.
Faith is Love believing.
Charity is Love acting.
Sacrifice is Love offering itself.
Patience is Love waiting.
Endurance is Love abiding.
Hope is Love expecting.
Peace is Love resting.
Prayer is Love communing.

Of all things you wear, your
expression is the most important.